Grandparenthood

More Than Rocking Chairs

Dr. Tim & Darcy Kimmel

family
matters

for every age and stage of life

for every age and stage of life

Family Matters™
P.O. Box 14382
Scottsdale, AZ 85267-4382
www.FamilyMatters.net
800.467.4596

Published by Family Matters™

Design by The M. Group, www.themgroupinc.com

Edited by Rance Meyers and Dawn Hutton Nassise

Printed in the United States of America

ISBN 0-9747683-2-4

*Grand*parenthood
More Than Rocking Chairs
Dr. Tim & Darcy Kimmel

family matters
for every age and stage of life

Grandparenthood *is* far more than rocking chairs. It is a second chance to do all of the "ought-tos" and "should-haves" that the busyness and demands of daily parenthood kept you from doing. It is living part of the idealistic dream of parenthood that real life, diapers, soccer practice, dance lessons, and waiting up for teenagers prevented you from doing. Grandparenthood allows you to play a key role in writing the history of a generation that you will some day leave in charge.

Together, you will learn how to:

- Pass on a great sense of blessing to each one of your grandchildren.
- Be a light to guide the way for the generations that follow you.
- Set a clear and reliable standard for your grandchildren to emulate.
- Help your grandchildren if and when their parents go through a divorce.
- Respond if your grandchildren move in with you.
- Be an effective grandparent to your step-grandchildren.
- "Spoil" your grandchildren in a positive way.
- Avoid crossing the fine line between intervening and interfering.
- Process the inevitable conflicts that go with grandparenting.
- Get even closer to your grandchildren as they grow older.
- Leave a legacy that lasts forever.

You are a very influential person! You may not realize it, but you are. As a grandparent, you have an opportunity to format young hearts and direct young minds in ways that will help them for a lifetime. Just by the mere fact that you are their grandparent, your grandchild sees you through a different set of eyes. They measure you by a different standard. They place a different emphasis on your words. More importantly, they place a higher priority on your actions. That is why none of us can afford to grandparent by accident.

Many grandparents want to use their position to make life-changing differences in their grandchildren. You can, too! This eight-part study is designed to equip you to be an even more strategic grandparent than you already are. All of us seem to improve our individual lives when we make a commitment to invest in others. This study is designed to help you see not only the "big picture" of grandparenting, but specific ways your life can impact each grandchild whom God has given to you to love.

As you go through this study, individual grandchildren are going to come to mind. You're going to think of ways that you can better fulfill your role as a mentor, leader, and ally to that grandchild. These thoughts might be prompted by something we say in the visual portion of the study or something that surfaces during the interactive discussion that follows. Our hope is that God will use these specific thoughts to encourage and inspire you to take action to be the most effective grandparent possible.

We look forward to being part of your life as you discover the grand joy of grandparenthood. It really is far more than rocking chairs.

Because your family matters,

Dr. Tim and Darcy Kimmel

Thank You. We We are delighted that you are going to lead this video/DVD
Appreciate You. series on Grandparenthood. You are going to have the opportunity to facilitate a study that will have a direct and profound
effect on many generations to come. It will also have a life-
changing affect on the grandparents who study along with you.

We are confident that the role you play as a facilitator will
enable many grandchildren to receive a much greater moral,
emotional, and spiritual foundation for the life that they will
ultimately live.

This Facilitator's Guide is designed to help you easily succeed
in your role. You will not only succeed, but you will find your
own life affected as well. During this series, grandparents are
going to laugh, cry, and make commitments to a whole new
standard of grandparenting.

We want to orient you to the material you will be using and
help you use this series in such a way that everyone participating will be able to embrace greater and grander roles as
leaders and mentors of their grandchildren. With that in
mind, let's go through a checklist for your success.

1. Determine a Format

One of the first things you need to do is to read all of this
introductory information, look over this Facilitator's Guide,
and then watch a couple of the lessons to get a feel for Tim
and Darcy Kimmel and how they present the material.

Once you've done this, you need to decide what your time
frame is going to be. If you are using this in a church setting,
you will have to adhere to a strict clock in order to get through
all of the parts of each lesson. If you are studying this in an
informal setting, like a home, you'll probably be able to give
more time to the discussion section of the study.

In an effort to be of assistance to you and to increase your enjoyment and success as you facilitate this video study, we have included facilitator prompts in this Facilitator's Guide. These are suggestions for you as you take the group through each session and lead the discussions. These facilitator prompts will be in a shaded box to set them apart from the participant's text and will appear only in this Facilitator's Guide.

Each lesson is broken down into 6 segments:

Grand Focus
Welcome everyone to the study, open in a brief prayer asking for God's help, give a brief review of the previous lesson, and a brief overview of the current lesson.
(1–2 minutes.)

Grand Principles
Dr. Kimmel and his wife, Darcy, teach the lesson via video/DVD while the participants fill in the outline in their workbooks. In the event that someone misses the words in the blanks as they are shown on the screen, the answers are in this Facilitator's Guide.
(22–28 minutes.)

Grand Precepts
This segment lets you take a closer look at supportive scripture.
(8–10 minutes.)

Grand Discussion
Spend some time responding to the discussion questions as a group. You are not required to discuss each one.
(12–15 minutes.)

Grand Priorities
This is the application part of the session, a chance to turn what you've learned into some practical points of action.
(5 minutes.)

Grand Power
Close off each session praying for the specific needs of the participant's grandchildren.

The above suggested time schedule is approximately 60 minutes and designed for a Sunday school format. If you only have an hour to work with, it's important to get right into the lesson. Besides the video/DVD teaching time, the other largest segments are the Grand Precepts and Grand Discussion times. In each Grand Precept segment there are two passages of scripture to look at. If your time is limited, you may choose to look at one in your group and then encourage them to study and respond to the other passage in their personal Bible study time later on in the week. There are four questions in each Grand Discussion. You may decide to limit your discussion to one or two of them.

If possible, the ideal time frame for this grandparenting study is 90 minutes. This time format is more probable in a home group study or individual study. If you have this much time to work with, you will be able to dedicate a lot more time to the Grand Precepts, Grand Discussion, and Grand Priorities segments of the lesson.

As you lead each session, there may be another question that is burning inside of you to be asked. Feel free to substitute your question or add to the ones that are already there. You may choose to spend more than one week on a particular lesson. Do what you think is best for the participants that you have and the time limitations you are working with.

2. Assure Effectiveness

Don't Work Alone — Recruit another person or couple to co-lead this study with you.

Order Workbooks — The Participant's Workbook is the most important tool in this video study. Every participant will gain much more from the study if they are following along with the teaching and discussion in their own personal workbook. The workbook is designed to increase the amount of information that they assimilate as well as enable them to tailor a strategy of grandparenting to their unique family situations.

Materials Fees — It's not uncommon to have a fee for materials when you are doing a video/DVD study in a church or home environment. If you are doing this study in a retreat setting, the cost of the workbook can easily be added to the fee for the weekend. Sometimes sponsors of the study are willing to pick up the cost. Regardless, the important point is that each participant has his or her own workbook. This increases their "take home" value dramatically.

Keep the Group Size Under Control — The ideal discussion size is 4 to 5 couples or 8 to 10 participants. If you are doing this study in a Sunday school or retreat setting, you should have the large group break down into smaller and more manageable groups. It is also more effective if the discussion groups are made up of the same individuals for the duration of the study.

Get The Word Out — Make sure that you publicize the study well enough in advance to get a good turnout. The CD-ROM in the back of this Facilitator's Guide has downloadable files to produce posters and bulletin inserts. If you do not have the computer hardware to print these items yourself, you can take the CD to your local print shop where they can help you.

Encourage Attendance — Although each lesson can stand by itself, the eight lessons together make up a complete picture of effective grandparenting. Once the study begins, encourage everyone to make the commitment to attend each lesson. This will not only enhance the value of the complete study for them, but also enable your group to develop deeper and more meaningful dialogue in the Grand Discussion section.

Encourage Individual Participation — This study will be more enjoyable if everyone gets involved in the discussion. Some people are naturally talkative while others are great listeners. You want to make sure that the "talkers" don't dominate the discussion while at the same time making sure that the "listeners" have a voice in the dialogue.

One way to get the "listeners" to share their insights is to direct a question to them that requires more than a "yes" or "no" answer.

Maintain Focus — It would be easy for the participants to go in many directions during the "Grand Discussion." It would also be easy for some of the questions to lead to a tangent that critiques parents, grandchildren, or the "in-law" set of grandparents. It's important that the sessions work toward helping the participants be more effective grandparents. You need to make sure the discussion stays focused on the question and the theme of that particular session by reminding them of the purpose of their discussion before they get started.

Application, Application, Application — The most important part of what you are doing is how it helps the participants become better grandparents. You want to make sure that you reserve enough time for them to respond to the Grand Priorities section of the lesson. This is usually done in quiet, with them coming up with at least one or two good applications that they'd like to take home and put into practice. This will be the greatest reward for you as a leader. Seeing grandparents allowing God to change them and make them more effective in their role is going to make all of your efforts worth it.

The Power of Prayer — The last section of your study is called "Grand Prayer." This is when you ask God for His help in taking what you've learned as a group and turning it into individual benefit. If you have the time, you might want to encourage requests regarding specific problems they are having within their extended families or specific prayer for a grandchild that has a particular need. This prayer time should be focused on their roles as grandparents and the individual needs of their grandchildren. It might be easy for this to be broadened to include all needs. It would be better if you schedule prayer for those kinds of issues at another time.

3. Give Them Something to Take Home

Additional Scripture — Besides the lesson, there are three other scriptural passages to draw their attention to: Grand Promise, Grand Proverb, and Grand Praise. Suggest that the participants commit one or more of these to memory or meditate on them throughout the week.

Grand Projects — There is a Grand Project for each lesson. These are designed to help the participants apply what they've learned in a very practical way and become a part of their relationship with their grandchildren. If time allows, ask some of the participants to report on how their Grand Project went each time you reconvene.

4. Group Commitments That Ensure Success
    (You might want to read these at the first meeting.)

Courtesy — Each participant should commit to arriving to each session on time.

Acceptance — Each participant should affirm the other participants' verbal contributions.

Confidentiality — Each participant should be careful to not talk about personal issues shared by fellow participants outside the context of this study.

Honesty — Each participant should be forthright and truthful when they speak.

Respect — Each participant should be careful not to stand in judgment, give quick advice, or criticize his or her fellow grandparents. The goal is to make the group a safe place for grandparents to talk openly about their roles and about their grandchildren.

5. Follow-up

Evaluations — When your group has completed the video series, ask each participant to fill in the evaluation found in the back of their workbook. Either collect all of them for mailing or encourage them to mail them to:

Family Matters™
P.O. Box 14382
Scottsdale, AZ 85267

Family Matters™ will send each participant that filled out a complete evaluation (including their address) a special reminder of their study together. Remember to mail them to Family Matters™ otherwise they will not receive their gift for participating.

Spread the Message Around — Encourage participants to lead their friends through a *Grandparenthood—More Than Rocking Chairs Video Study*. This will not only enable more grandparents to become more effective in their roles, but it will also enable the person leading the study to grow in his or her role as a grandparent as well. If they would like to order a video or DVD study, encourage them to go to the Family Matters™ web site at www.familymatters.net, or call toll-free 800.467.4596.

A Grandparenting Reunion — You might want to have a reunion of your group six months after you have completed your study in order to get updates on how they are doing as grandparents as well as to spend time praying for each other's grandchildren.

We appreciate you! May God richly bless you for your willingness to lead *Grandparenthood—More Than Rocking Chairs*.

Tim & Darcy

Tim and Darcy Kimmel

SESSION 1

Grand focus

In this session, Tim and Darcy Kimmel remind us that grandparenthood is a strategic privilege. They will paint a picture of the modern grandparent and will point out the many assets grandparents bring to families today. They will also draw attention to some of the "sacred cows" that undermine our ability to be the kind of grandparents we'd all like to be.

Welcome everyone. Congratulate them on their desire to be better grandparents. Since this is the first session, this might be a good time to go around the circle and find out how many grandchildren everyone has. If you are using this in a Sunday School class or a retreat setting, you may want to divide the participants into smaller groups in order to do this more quickly (5–6 persons per group). It is important to keep a close eye on your watch. You want to save as much time as possible for interaction and application. Once you've welcomed everyone, pray and ask for God's help and insight as all of you watch the video/DVD and then discuss and apply it. After you have prayed, read the Grand Focus statement at the beginning of this session, start the video/DVD and have them follow along in their workbooks.

It is important that everyone has a good view of the TV or screen and that everyone has a workbook. As the session starts, make sure that the audio is at a level that everyone can hear.

Grand principles

Please follow along with Tim and Darcy on the video/DVD and fill in the blanks as they teach. The phrases with blanks will come up on the screen.

Grandparenting: A Grand Love

A. Grandparenting is like giving you a _second_ _chance_ to impact a child's life well.

B. Grandparenting is a _sacred_ _trust_ .

A New Generation of Grandparents

A. This generation of grandparents is the best _educated_ , most active and youngest "older" generation that has ever existed.

B. The new challenge our grandchildren will face will not be whether we can keep up with them, but whether they can keep up with _us_ .

III The Assets of Effective Grandparents

A. Asset 1: <u>Maturity</u>

    1. Maturity is the result of a deliberate decision to learn from life.

    2. It helps us draw better conclusions, more careful assumptions, and more tempered suppositions when we're facing the <u>future</u>.

    3. Our children and grandchildren desperately need parents who consider it a mandate to act like grownups.

B. Asset 2: <u>Experience</u>

    1. Our experiences provide <u>clout</u> when we offer advice.

    2. Experience enables us to whisper a <u>wiser</u> encouragement into our grandchildren's ears when life seems to be getting the best of them.

C. Asset 3: <u>Perspective</u>

    1. Perspective not only gives us more <u>objectivity</u>, it lends itself to a more accurate sense of retrospection.

    2. Perspective helps us use the past to evaluate the present so that we can make more <u>sober choices</u> in the future.

D. Asset 4: <u>Assistance</u>

    1. Our children need us to be able to assist them with <u>time</u>.

    2. <u>Relief</u> comes by walking alongside them when they're discouraged, exhausted, or sick in order to help them carry their heavy burden of parenting.

3. We can offer assistance by being a _sounding board_ that lets them try out ideas regarding their roles as parents.

4. The other resource that our children may occasionally need assistance with is _money_ .

E.   Asset 5: _Love_

1. Love is what _motivates_ us to offer all of our other assets.

2. Many times "grandparenting love" is as close to _unconditional_ love as a human can get.

3. Love is the _commitment_ of my will to your needs and best interests, regardless of the cost.

Looking at a Few Sacred Cows

A.   Sacred Cow #1: _Empty Nest_

1. Just because our children are grown and gone doesn't mean we cease to be _parents_ .

2. Using the empty nest as a license to indulge ourselves to the exclusion of our families shows a level of rejection towards our children and grandchildren that can do incredible _harm_ .

B.   Sacred Cow #2: _Retirement_

1. God never meant for us to see our twilight years as a time to put our lives on cruise control and not be involved in making life _significant_ to the people who matter most to us.

2. Retirement is a time to move up to the responsibility of being a _patriarch_ and a _matriarch_ .

Make sure everyone has the words for the blanks in their workbook.

Grand precepts

This is an opportunity for you to dig deeper into the scriptures and be reminded of God's work in your life.

Introduce this section by saying something like, "Let's spend a few minutes looking more closely at what God's Word has to say about putting the grand back in parenting." Have someone read the referenced scripture and then encourage them to discuss the questions in their group.

Psalms 71:17, 18

"Since my youth, O God, you have taught me, and to this day I declare your marvelous deeds. And even when I am old and gray, do not forsake me, O God, until I declare your power to the next generation, your might to all who are to come."

1. As you look back on your life, share at least one way that God has taught you how marvelous He is.

   His grace, His mercy, how He brought them to know Him personally, the way God has brought them through hardship, the wonderful things He has done in their families, the way He has changed them.

2. What are some specific examples of God's power and God's might that you want to declare to your grandchildren?

   They might mention God's faithfulness in their careers, their marriages, their health, their finances, their relationships with people and friends. They might mention the way He has preserved them through frightening experiences like combat, an accident, or an illness.

John 15:12, 13 "My command is this: Love each other as I have loved you. Greater love has no man than this, that he lay down his life for his friends."

1. List three or four adjectives that describe God's love for us. How can we show this same kind of love to our children and grandchildren?

   His love is long-suffering, unconditional, sacrificial, and unselfish.

2. Our culture suggests that we view the years after we have raised our children as a time to indulge ourselves— sometimes at the expense of our children and grandchildren. What does this verse say about that attitude?

   A self-indulgent attitude doesn't reflect the kind of love God has toward us. Jesus was willing to die for us. The least we can do is be willing to live for the best interests of our extended family.

Grand discussion

This is your opportunity to share your experience and perspective, as well as do some new thinking on our grandparenthood topic.

1. Of the five assets (Maturity, Experience, Perspective, Assistance, and Love), which one do you feel most qualified to give? Which one do you feel your children need most from you?

2. Since you've become a grandparent, what sacrifices have you had to make in order to carry out your role as an effective asset to your children and your grandchildren?

Helping with childcare, occasional financial help, rearranging schedules, moving closer to the grandchildren. Some may even talk about having to be the primary caregiver.

3. As you look at our culture's attitude toward an "empty nest" and the retirement years, in what ways do you think it is antagonistic toward your carrying out your godly roles as grandparents?

Retirement communities often discourage the regular contact and interaction with grandchildren. They also encourage a more indulgent attitude toward being a "senior" member of society—often at the expense of effective grandparenting. Having second homes that take us far from our children and grandchildren for long blocks of time or traveling for extended periods of time need to be considered against the backdrop of our greater calling as grandparents.

4. Sometimes our desire for freedom from the responsibilities of parenting causes us to neglect our role as grandparents. Have you seen any of these tendencies in your own life?

Grand . .
priorities

This is your opportunity to apply what you have learned in this session and become an even better grandparent.

This is the most important part of the session. Make sure you allow enough time for the participants to make personal applications from what they have learned.

Questions that
make me think:

1. How has this session challenged my thinking and perspective of grandparenthood?

    _____
    _____

2. What is one new concept or idea that comes out of this session that will change my priorities as a grandparent?

    _____
    _____

Actions that
make me change:

1. With God's help, I will commit to making these changes in my own life:

    _____
    _____

2. With God's help, I will commit to the following action(s) toward those I love:

    _____
    _____

Make sure that you point out the Grand Promise, Grand Proverb, Grand Praise, and Grand Project at the end of Grand Priorities before you close in prayer with Grand Power.

# Grand power

Close this session by praying for your grandchildren, especially regarding your ability to come alongside them with the assets of maturity, experience, perspective, assistance, and love.

Grand Promise
Philippians 2:3, 4

"Do nothing out of selfish ambition or vain conceit, but in humility consider others better than yourselves. Each of you should look not only to your own interests, but also to the interests of others."

Grand Proverb
Proverbs 16:31

"Gray hair is a crown of splendor; it is attained by a righteous life."

Grand Praise
1 Thessalonians
5:16-18

"Be joyful always; pray continually; give thanks in all circumstances, for this is God's will for you in Christ Jesus."

Blessings often put burdens in perspective. Based on this session, what are some of the things for which you are thankful when it comes to your relationships with your children and grandchildren?

_____

_____

_____

_____

Grand project

Putting the Grand in Parenting

Show your grandchildren a photo of yourself when you were a child. Let them tell you the resemblances and differences they see between the photograph and how you look now.

Either have them draw a picture or give a verbal description of what they imagine themselves looking like when they are grandparents.

Grand Love…
the natural connection that grandparents have with
their grandchildren.

Love…
the commitment of my will to your needs and best interests
regardless of the cost.

Grandparenthood…
a second chance to do all of the "ought-tos" and "should-
haves" that the busyness and demands of daily parenthood
kept you from doing. It is living part of the idealistic dream
of parenthood that real life, diapers, soccer practice, dance lessons, and waiting up for teenagers prevented you from doing.

Recommended Little House on the Freeway
Reading *by Dr. Tim Kimmel*

For a deeper look at how to maintain calm and rest in the
midst of your busy families, you might want to read Dr. Tim
Kimmel's book, *Little House on the Freeway*, available online
at www.familymatters.net or call 800 467-4596.

Giving
a Blessing

Grand focus

In our last session we learned about the five greatest assets we bring to our roles as grandparents: our maturity, our experiences, our perspective, our assistance, and our love. In this session, Tim and Darcy Kimmel will show us how to give a blessing to our grandchildren by helping meet the three driving inner needs of their hearts.

Welcome everyone and recognize any new members of the study. Mention to them that this session is going to cover an area that might have been a void in their own childhood. The great thing about learning God's truth is that there is always something in it for us. It's also nice to know that it is never too late to learn how to be used by God to do great things in the lives of our grandchildren. Pray for God's help and understanding. Read the Grand Focus statement at the beginning of this session and then turn on the session.

It is important that everyone has a good view of the TV or screen and that everyone has a workbook. As the session starts, make sure that the audio is at a level that everyone can hear.

Grand principles

Please follow along with Tim and Darcy on the video/DVD and fill in the blanks as they teach. The words for the blanks will come up on the screen.

Helping Your Grandchildren Develop a ...

The three needs that every child is born with are the need for a secure <u>love</u> , the need for a significant <u>purpose</u> , and the need for a sufficient <u>hope</u> .

...Secure Love

A. Grandchildren feel a secure love when they know their grandparents <u>accept</u> them as they are.

B. Grandchildren feel a secure love through a close <u>affiliation</u> with a loving and honoring family.

C. Grandchildren feel a secure love when they receive regular and generous helpings of <u>affection</u> .

...Significant Purpose

A. Grandchildren feel a significant purpose when they are regularly <u>affirmed</u> .

B. Grandchildren feel a significant purpose when they know they have our <u>attention</u> .

Grand Principles, C. Grandchildren feel a significant purpose when we
continued   gracefully _admonish_ them.

...Sufficient A. Grandchildren feel a sufficient hope when we help them
Hope   recognize their God-given _abilities_ and develop them.

B. Grandchildren feel a sufficient hope when we
   encourage them to live a life of _adventure_ .

C. Grandchildren feel a sufficient hope when we
   help them turn their childhood into a series of
   positive _accomplishments_ .

Conclusion A checklist of practical things you can do to bless your
             grandchildren spiritually, emotionally, and physically.

A. Blessing Them Spiritually

   1. _Pray_ for them.

   2. Show them how to grow in their faith and use their
      spiritual gifts.

B. Blessing Them Emotionally

   1. Celebrate their _accomplishments_ .

   2. Avoid showing _favoritism_ .

C. Blessing Them Physically

   1. Provide a safe and comfortable home where they
      are always _welcome_ .

   2. Assure them that they are beautiful or handsome in
      our sight, as well as _God's_ .

This is an opportunity for you to dig deeper into the scriptures and be reminded of God's work in your life.

Make sure that everyone has all of the blanks filled in properly. Have one of the participants read the scripture and then walk them through the questions. If time is limited, you may choose to study one of the passages or answer just one question per passage. If you choose to do this, encourage participants to spend time answering the other questions themselves in their personal Bible studies.

Psalm 128 "Blessed are all who fear the LORD, who walk in his ways. You will eat the fruit of your labor; blessings and prosperity will be yours. Your wife will be like a fruitful vine within your house; your sons will be like olive shoots around your table. Thus is the man blessed who fears the LORD. May the LORD bless you from Zion all the days of your life; may you see the prosperity of Jerusalem, and may you live to see your children's children. Peace be upon Israel."

1. What do you feel is the connection between having a healthy "fear" of the Lord and being blessed in life?

    Fearing God keeps us from fearing the things of this world that might intimidate us. Fearing God keeps us from giving in to the thinking of our culture and making poor choices that cause problems in our lives, i.e., wrong attitudes toward money, conflict, selfishness, and overall relationships. Fearing God keeps us from sinning. Sin often blocks God's blessing in our lives.

2. What kind of prosperity do you think the Psalmist is referring to?

> Prosperity in the Bible generally refers to richness in relationships, a better reputation, a greater sense of eternal accomplishment, and contentment in our position in life. The Psalmist is not necessarily referring to wealth or ease.

3. How do you think our respect and love for the Lord translates into specific blessings to our grandchildren?

> We have a better role model. God is more inclined to respond to our prayers on behalf of our grandchildren (1 Peter 3:7 teaches that sin in our marriage blocks our prayers to God, and 1 Peter 3:8-12 makes the same point in a broader context of relationships), God promises to bless the offspring of righteous people (Deuteronomy 7:9). Godly grandparents simply make better grandparents.

1 Thessalonians
5:23, 24 "May God himself, the God of peace, sanctify you through and through. May your whole spirit, soul, and body be kept blameless at the coming of our Lord Jesus Christ. The one who calls you is faithful and he will do it."

Commentary As Paul closed his letter to the church in Thessalonica, he wanted to send them off with a blessing. Notice that he addressed the three inner needs of their hearts that Tim and Darcy referred to in this session. "Sanctify" means to set apart for a special purpose — "a significant purpose." "May your whole spirit, soul, body …" refers to a security that they enjoy because they are loved by God. "The One who calls is faithful and He will do it" refers to the sufficient hope that is theirs because of their relationship with Christ.

1. How does finding your love, purpose, and hope in God help you meet these needs in your grandchildren?

   Grandchildren see what it looks like to have these needs met through Christ. Our example will always stand in distinct contrast to the world's way of meeting these needs. Grandchildren can trust our advice and counsel when they see that it is backed up by our lifestyle. Because we know how to have these needs met in our own lives through an authentic relationship with Christ, we know what it takes to meet them in our grandchildren's lives.

2. What special purposes do you feel you've been set aside for in your grandchildren's lives?

   There could be many great answers to this question.

Grand discussion

This is your opportunity to share your experience and perspective, as well as do some new thinking on our grandparenthood topic.

1. How does our culture encourage our grandchildren to meet their inner needs for Love, Purpose, and Hope?

   Love: material possessions, sex, and money. Purpose: popularity, looks, applause, recognition. Hope: power, high-control, careers, connections.

2. What have you found to be some of the difficult challenges of accepting your grandchildren as they are?

> What my friends will think of them. Their strange styles and tastes. Their annoying music. Their inadequacies. Their parents. Their quirky personalities. Their irritating habits. Their lack of spiritual interests.

3. When it comes to admonishing (cautioning or disciplining) your grandchildren, what responsibilities (if any) do you feel you have as a grandparent?

> Some might think that disciplining is not our job. We might feel that we are the only ones that are doing any admonishing of the grandchildren and therefore feel discouraged. We might feel that we are coming up against the grandchildren's parents.

4. Why do grandparents so often struggle with showing favoritism? How do you think showing favoritism affects your relationship with the parents of your grandchildren?

> We are automatically closer to the grandchildren who live nearer simply because we can see them more often. We may get along better with one set of parents. There are ages/genders/personalities that we tend to gravitate to. Similar interests. Our favoritism can only exasperate the parents and the grandchildren that are slighted.

Grand. .
priorities

This is your opportunity to apply what you have learned in this session and become an even better grandparent.

This is the most important part of the session. Make sure you allow enough time for the participants to make personal applications from what they have learned.

Questions that make me think:

1. How has this session challenged my thinking and perspective of grandparenthood?

   _____

   _____

2. What is one new concept or idea that comes out of this session that will transform my priorities as a grandparent?

   _____

   _____

Actions that make me change:

1. With God's help, I will commit to making these changes in my own life:

   _____

   _____

2. With God's help, I will commit to the following action(s) toward those I love:

   _____

   _____

Make sure that you point out the Grand Promise, Grand Proverb, Grand Praise, and Grand Project at the end of Grand Priorities before you close in prayer with Grand Power.

Grand power

Close this session by praying for your grandchildren, especially regarding your ability to meet their three inner needs for a secure love, a significant purpose, and a sufficient hope.

Grand Promise
Ephesians 4:29

"Do not let any unwholesome talk come out of your mouths, but only what is helpful for building others up according to their needs, that it may benefit those who listen."

Grand Proverb
Proverbs 10:7a

"The memory of the righteous will be a blessing."

Grand Praise
Psalm 146:2

"I will praise the LORD all of my life; I will sing praise to my God as long as I live."

Blessings often put burdens in perspective. Based on this session, what are some of the things for which you are thankful when it comes to your relationship with your children and grandchildren?

_____

_____

_____

_____

Grand project

Giving a Blessing

If you haven't already, start a prayer journal for your grandchildren. See the back of your workbook for an example. If your grandchildren are old enough, ask them what you can pray about for them in the three areas mentioned in the session (spiritually, emotionally, and physically).

As your grandchildren grow up it will be a great testimony of God's faithfulness to be able to show them how God has answered your prayers and theirs.

Secure Love…
a combination of our acceptance, affiliation, and affection that helps our grandchildren find their true love in Christ.

Significant Purpose…
a combination of our affirmation, attention, and admonition that helps our grandchildren find their true purpose in Christ.

Sufficient Hope…
a combination of our recognition of their abilities, our encouragement of their sense of adventure, and our aid in assisting them in putting together a series of positive accomplishments that helps our grandchildren find their true hope in Christ.

SESSION 3

Grand focus

In our last session we learned the first primary role of a grandparent—giving a blessing. We learned how to give our grandchildren a blessing by helping to meet their three most important inner needs: their need for a secure love, their need for a significant purpose, and their need for a sufficient hope. In this session, Tim and Darcy Kimmel will show us how to leave a legacy that lasts forever.

Make sure everyone has a workbook and a pen. After welcoming everyone and praying for God to give your group great insight into leaving a legacy, read the Grand Focus statement at the beginning of this session, and then play Session 3.

It is important that everyone has a good view of the TV or screen and that everyone has a workbook. As the session starts, make sure that the audio is at a level that everyone can hear.

Grand principles

Please follow along with Tim and Darcy on the video/DVD and fill in the blanks as they teach. The phrases with blanks will come up on the screen.

Leaving a legacy can be complicated because:

- We didn't have good role models when we were younger.

- We didn't know the Lord until we were much older.

- We *did* know God when we were younger but neglected to make our daily choices according to the mandates of His <u>Word</u>.

Restoring a Lost Legacy

A. We need to ask God to forgive <u>us</u>.

B. We need to forgive <u>ourselves</u>.

C. We need to ask our <u>children</u> for forgiveness.

The Benefits of Seeking Forgiveness

A. We take steps to relieve the <u>tension</u> between our children and ourselves.

B. It frees our children up to be <u>better</u> parents to our grandchildren.

C. It strengthens the kind of _influence_ we get to have on our grandchildren.

D. We've got to be diligent to make sure that we keep our relationships _reconciled_ .

A Legacy That Lasts Forever

A. Work overtime to bring _honor_ to our family's reputation.

1. They need to see people whose "yeses" are "Yes!" and whose "nos" are "No!"

2. The rules and guidelines in your home need to _reinforce_ , rather than undermine, their parents'.

B. Make our daily decisions with an _eternal_ perspective in mind.

1. Our grandchildren need to see our consistent _confidence_ in the salvation we have in Jesus Christ.

2. We need to take opportunities to remind them of how God has been faithful to us, how He continues to show us His goodness, and how He _empowers_ us to endure through suffering and hardship.

3. They need to see grandparents who _love_ people and _use_ things, not the other way around.

C. Leave _clear_ _tracks_ for our grandchildren to follow.

1. They need to see us choosing grace.

2. They need to see us backing up our words with actions.

3. They need to see us avoiding cynicism.

4. They need to see us demonstrating <u>faithful</u> living.

Grand precepts *This is an opportunity for you to dig deeper into the scriptures and be reminded of God's work in your life.*

Psalm 78:2b-7 "I will utter hidden things, things from of old—what we have heard and known, what our fathers have told us. We will not hide them from their children; we will tell the next generation the praiseworthy deeds of the Lord, his power, and the wonders he has done. He decreed statutes for Jacob and established the law in Israel, which he commanded our forefathers to teach their children, so the next generation would know them, even the children yet to be born, and they in turn would tell their children. Then they would put their trust in God and would not forget his deeds but would keep his commands."

1. Why do you think God put so much emphasis on His followers passing down the stories about His "praiseworthy deeds" to the next generation?

   We are forgetful. A positive track record encourages people who are ready to give up to keep hanging on. It encourages both the one hearing about the story of God's faithfulness as well as the one telling about it.

2. Do you think your family has done a good job of this? Why or why not?

Ephesians 4:31, 32 "Get rid of all bitterness, rage and anger, brawling and slander, along with every form of malice. Be kind and compassionate to one another, forgiving each other, just as in Christ God forgave you."

1. Do you find these verses easy to obey when it comes to your children and grandchildren? Why or why not?

2. How does remembering the things for which you have been forgiven help you to forgive others?

    An honest assessment of our own sin keeps us humble. Humility gives us more patience with others who fall short. It reminds us of how loved we are, in spite of our unworthiness. It helps us view each other the way God views us—with grace and mercy.

Grand discussion

This is your opportunity to share your experience and perspective, as well as do some new thinking on our grandparenthood topic.

1. What kind of spiritual legacy were you given by your parents and grandparents? What impact does this have on your ability to pass on a godly legacy to your grandchildren?

    Regarding impact: having received a good spiritual legacy clearly makes it easier for us to leave a good legacy of our own. If we inherited a bad spiritual legacy, this gives us a great opportunity to show just how powerful God's love really is. Our changed lives point to His mercy, His grace, and His love.

2. Assuming that none of us were perfect parents, what part of your relationship with your children (your legacy) needs to be repaired? What makes this difficult for you to do?

   Regarding the second question: Often our pride gets in the way. Sometimes our children are unwilling to even talk to us about these issues. Maybe we've tried in the past but our children have reacted in anger—attacking us with hurtful words. They see things far worse than we see them.

3. How is your relationship with your daughter-in-law or son-in-law affecting your ability to leave a godly legacy to your grandchildren?

4. What are some subtle ways that we can mislead our grandchildren into thinking that things are more important than people?

   Showing them less attention than they would prefer because of our hobbies or personal interests. Displaying so much value on the care of our home/possessions that when they come over we don't allow them to 'just be kids.' Allowing market adjustments, poor return on investments, or the deterioration of possessions steal our joy. We spend so much time on our own indulgences that we have little time for helping others.

Grand . .
priorities
This is your opportunity to apply what you have learned in this session and become an even better grandparent.

This is the most important part of the session. Make sure you allow enough time for the participants to make personal applications from what they have learned.

Questions that
make me think:

1. How has this session challenged my thinking and perspective of grandparenthood?

   _____

   _____

2. What is one new concept or idea that comes out of this session that will change my priorities as a grandparent?

   _____

   _____

Actions that
make me change:

1. With God's help, I will commit to making these changes in my own life:

   _____

   _____

2. With God's help, I will commit to the following action(s) toward those I love:

   _____

   _____

Make sure that you point out the Grand Promise, Grand Proverb, Grand Praise, and Grand Project at the end of this application and before you close in prayer.

Grand
power

Close this session by praying for your grandchildren, especially regarding your ability to leave a legacy that inspires them to live a greater and more spiritually productive life.

Grand Promise
Galatians 6:9

"Let us not become weary in doing good, for at the proper time we will reap a harvest if we do not give up."

Grand Proverb
Proverbs 20:7

"The righteous man leads a blameless life; blessed are his children after him."

Grand Praise
Jude 24, 25

"To him who is able to keep you from falling and to present you before his glorious presence without fault and with great joy—to the only God our Savior be glory, majesty, power and authority, through Jesus Christ our Lord, before all ages, now and forever more! Amen."

Blessings often put burdens in perspective. Based on this session, what are some of the things for which you are thankful when it comes to your relationship with your children and grandchildren?

_____

_____

_____

_____

Grand project

Leaving a Legacy

Gather together as many symbols of your life's legacy as possible (i.e., photos, medals, citations, certificates, collections, letters, a well-worn Bible, etc.). Show them to your grandchildren and have them choose one for you to tell them about. Explain how this part of your life helped mold you into what you are today.

Ask your grandchildren to choose a symbol of their accomplishments or priorities in life and to tell you about what it means to them (i.e., report card, Scouting medal, dance shoes, trophy, completed book, toy, etc.). Let them know how proud you are of them. Remind them that they are starting to develop the legacy that they will some day give to their family.

Grand words

Legacy…
the message that your actions and words leave to the next generation.

Forgiveness…
the relinquishing of your right to get even and stay mad at someone.

Eating Crow…
refers to a process of swallowing your pride, admitting your guilt, and asking for forgiveness. Generally, it leaves no bitter aftertaste.

Epitaph…
a single phrase that captures the sum-total of your life.

Dr. Tim & Darcy Kimmel

Bearing
a Torch

Grand focus

In our last session we learned the second primary role of a
grandparent—leaving a godly legacy. We learned about the
powerful role of forgiveness and reconciliation in restoring
broken legacies. We also learned how to bring honor to our
family's reputation, how to make daily decisions from an eternal
perspective, and how to leave clear tracks for our grandchildren
to follow. In this session, Tim and Darcy Kimmel will show
us how to be torchbearers of God's love and grace.

Welcome everyone. Thank them for their faithfulness to the study. Give one example from your own life of how this study has already helped you. Pray for God's help and insight as you go through this session together. Read the Grand Focus statement at the beginning of this session and then start the video/DVD.

It is important that everyone has a good view of the TV or screen and that everyone has a workbook. As the session starts, make sure that the audio is at a level that everyone can hear.

Grand principles

Please follow along with Tim and Darcy on the video/DVD and fill in the blanks as they speak. The phrases with blanks will come up on the screen.

Torchbearers of the Gospel

A. We need to make sure our grandchildren <u>hear</u> the gospel.

B. We must trust the Holy Spirit to draw them to Himself on His <u>timetable</u> .

C. We need to demonstrate a consistent <u>concern</u> and <u>compassion</u> for those grandchildren who have chosen at this point not to give their lives to Christ.

Torchbearers of Moral Living

A. Grandchildren need to see us <u>flourishing</u> within the hostile culture that surrounds us.

B. Grandchildren need to see grandparents who take bold yet gracious <u>stands</u> on moral issues.

C. Grandchildren need to see grandparents who show them how to develop <u>discernment</u> and make right choices.

A. We put them _down_ .

    1. By _distancing_ ourselves from them.

    2. By forcing them to _defend_ all the things about themselves and their culture that we don't like.

    3. By treating them the _opposite_ _way_ Jesus would deal with their unique features and their culture.

B. We _ignore_ them.

    1. By not wanting to be _seen_ with them.

    2. By being so disgusted by their culture that we simply _write_ _them_ _off_ .

C. We _imitate_ them.

    1. By trying to _look_ like them.

    2. By trying to _act_ like them.

    3. By trying to _reason_ like them.

Grand precepts

This is an opportunity for you to dig deeper into the scriptures and be reminded of God's work in your life.

Matthew 5:14-16   "You are the light of the world. A city on a hill cannot be hidden. Neither do people light a lamp and put it under a bowl. Instead they put it on its stand, and it gives light to everyone in the house. In the same way, let your light shine before men, that they may see your good deeds and praise your Father in heaven."

1. What are some of the ways we might unwittingly put our light under a bowl (or bushel basket) as grandparents?

    Not praying at meals or making the Bible a central part of our daily lives when we are around our grandchildren. Being reluctant to refer to God or His work in our lives when we are around them.

    What are some of the ways we can put it on a stand for everyone in our house to see (without being obnoxious)?

    Having consistent joy (not necessarily happiness) through the highs and lows of life. Being compassionate and caring for others. Looking out for the best interests of people who are weak or helpless. Not being ashamed to tell others what God has done in our lives. Not condemning people who are lost and clueless about the things of the Spirit.

2. Verse 16 talks about doing "good deeds" in such a way as it would cause people to "praise your Father in heaven." How can we do good deeds in a way in which God will end up getting the glory for them instead of us?

> Not worry whether or not people know what we did, or whether they go out of their way to thank us personally for what we did. Do good things when it is a huge imposition for us to do it. Do good things with a joyful spirit.

3. What kind of things (actions/attitudes/words) in our lives would cause our grandchildren to be thankful to God for how He is working through us?

> They see a genuine humility, joy, and sacrifice in how we go about doing good things for others. They notice in us a gratefulness in being able to serve others as well as a lack of concern about whether or not we get recognition or credit for what we have done.

Matthew 18:5, 6 "And whoever welcomes a little child like this in my name welcomes me. But if anyone causes one of these little ones who believes in me to sin, it would be better for him to have a large millstone hung around his neck and to be drowned in the depths of the sea."

1. Why do you think God is so harsh toward adults who would cause children to stumble?

> Adults should know better. Children are completely dependent on us. Children place their trust in us. God places great value on "childlike" faith. We should not devalue it by causing them to stumble. Misleading them could cause them pain and suffering for the rest of their lives.

2. What are some of the ways well-intended grandparents might place a stumbling block in front of their grandchild?

Pushing Jesus down their throats. Not showing sensitivity for their age, tastes, and interests. Having unrealistic expectations regarding their level of spiritual maturity. Being a poor role model.

Grand *discussion*

This is your opportunity to share your experience and perspective, as well as do some new thinking on our grandparenthood topic.

1. As most believers become older, have you observed that they spend more time trying to reach out to non-believers, or do they tend to increasingly just focus on their Christian relationships? Explain.

Many believers as they get into the later stages of life tend to spend time almost exclusively with believing friends because it is more comfortable to do so. However, there are tremendous opportunities for mature Christians to make an impact on non-Christians—young and old alike.

2. How does our attitude toward the unbelieving world help determine how our grandchildren view the unbelieving world around them?

When they see how confident we are in God and therefore how unafraid we are of the lost world around us, it gives them courage to follow the same path we are taking as they work their way through their own corrupted culture.

3. How can grandparents be guilty of being too pushy when it comes to transferring their beliefs to their grand-children? Why do you think some grandparents do this?

   Matthew 10:16. We react to external things about their lifestyle that annoy us or offend us without connecting to their hearts. We become unwilling to wait on the Holy Spirit to draw their hearts to Him on His timetable. We ambush or browbeat them about spiritual things or "push" spiritual behavior on them.

4. Tim and Darcy mentioned three mistakes that grandpar-ents can make when it comes to our attitudes toward our grandchildren: we put them down, we ignore them, or we imitate them. Of these three, which one (if any) do you struggle with the most?

Grand priorities

This is your opportunity to apply what you have learned in this session and become an even better grandparent.

This is the most important part of the session. Make sure you allow enough time for the participants to make personal appli-cations from what they have learned.

Questions that
make me think:

1. How has this session challenged my thinking and perspective of grandparenthood?

   _____

   _____

2. What is one new concept or idea that comes out of this session that will change my priorities as a grandparent?

   _____

   _____

   _____

Actions that make me change:

1. With God's help, I will commit to making these changes in my own life:

    _____

    _____

2. With God's help, I will commit to the following action(s) toward those I love:

    _____

    _____

Make sure that you point out the Grand Promise, Grand Proverb, Grand Praise, and Grand Project at the end of this application and before you close in prayer.

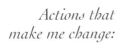

power

Close this session by praying for your grandchildren, especially regarding your spiritual influence on them. Pray that God helps you be a steady and sure light to their finding the right path to God. Also, pray that God will help you avoid the mistakes of putting down their culture, ignoring them as young people, or not being the mature example they need.

Grand Promise
John 8:12

"I am the light of the world. Whoever follows me will never walk in darkness, but will have the light of life."

Grand Proverb
Proverbs 16:3

"Commit to the LORD whatever you do, and your plans will succeed."

Grand Praise
John 3:21

"But whoever lives by the truth comes into the light, so that it may be seen plainly that what he has done has been done through God."

Grand Power,
continued

Blessings often put burdens in perspective. Based on this session, what are some of the things for which you are thankful when it comes to your relationship with your children and grandchildren?

_____

_____

_____

_____

Grand project

This project requires risk. Pray for God's wisdom, patience, and grace before you do this project.

Bearing a Torch

In order to understand your grandchildren's world better as well as build a deeper connection to their hearts, have them pick out their favorite movie or their favorite music CD (lyrical). Watch the movie with them or have them play their favorite song from the CD. Listen with the idea to hear the true message that the movie or musical artist is trying to communicate. Even if you end up not liking the movie or CD, try to find some things that you can compliment about it—since to say something good about what your grandchildren like is to say something good about them. Without condemnation (cp. John 3:16-17) ask them questions about the primary message, the conflict, or the conclusions that the movie or music offers. Discuss with your grandchild what he or she thinks is the world view behind the movie or song (the spiritual presuppositions that the writer/performer embraces).

Ask them how they think Jesus would respond to the needs of these people in the movie or the concern addressed within the song. Don't look on this as an opportunity to critique their tastes or to fix their faulty thinking, but rather as a time to show them how much you care about them as a young person. This is also a great opportunity to show them how Jesus' life and message relates to all people's problems. (Qualification: If your grandchild wants you to watch or listen to something that is utterly odious to you, you should ask them for an alternative.)

Grand words

Torchbearer...
one who goes before and lights the way for those who follow.
One who holds up a light for everyone to see.

World View...
refers to the spiritual presuppositions through which they
filter daily life and that format their actions and convictions.

Gospel...
the good news of God's love, mercy, forgiveness, and grace
made possible through Christ's sacrifice on the cross.

Setting
a Standard

SESSION 5

 Grand focus

In our last session we learned the third primary role of a grandparent — bearing a torch for our grandchildren. We also looked at three mistakes that grandparents often make that undermine their ability to bear a torch of God's love for their grandchildren. In this session, Tim and Darcy Kimmel will show us the fourth primary role of a grandparent — setting a good standard for our grandchildren to emulate.

If you can get a hand-held GPS (global positioning satellite system) it would make a great prop for introducing this lesson. (Some people have these on their palm pilots. You might want to check with your children or grandchildren to see if they might have one you can borrow for this lesson.) After you welcome everyone, take one minute to tell a story of either how one of your grandparents set a good standard for you, or how you have been called on to set a specific standard for one of your own grandchildren. Show them the GPS system, maybe even have it set on the exact address where you are doing the study and mention to them that this is the piece of equipment that Tim and Darcy are going to be making reference to in the beginning of their session. Pray for God's wisdom, for insight into the content of the lesson, and for His help in applying it into your lives. Read the Grand Focus statement at the beginning of this session and then begin the session with Tim and Darcy.

It is important that everyone has a good view of the TV or screen and that everyone has a workbook. As the session starts, make sure that the audio is at a level that everyone can hear.

Grand principles

Please follow along with Tim and Darcy on the video/DVD and fill in the blanks as they teach. The phrases with blanks will come up on the screen.

Setting a Standard of Clear Moral Absolutes

A. They are growing up in a world that has placed the importance of <u>feelings</u> over decency.

B. Today's culture assumes that we all have the freedom to create whatever <u>morality</u> is convenient to us.

C. We have all been affected by the <u>relativism</u> of the culture that surrounds us.

Grand Principles,	D.	Our grandchildren need to see grandparents who look
continued		past the (cultural) storms on the horizon and who see
		instead a mighty, sovereign God who has everything
		<u>under</u> <u>control</u> .

Setting a Standard	A.	We need to model the character trait of a
of Well-developed		contagious <u>faith</u> .
and Balanced		
Character	B.	We need to model the character trait of a
		consistent <u>integrity</u> .

C. We need to model the character trait of a
practical <u>poise</u> .

D. We need to model the character trait of a
personal <u>discipline</u> .

E. We need to model the character trait of a
steadfast <u>endurance</u> .

F. We need to model the character trait of an
inspirational <u>courage</u> .

Grand precepts

This is an opportunity for you to dig deeper into the scriptures and be reminded of God's work in your life.

Philippians 4:8, 9 "Finally brothers, whatever is true, whatever is noble, whatever is right, whatever is pure, whatever is lovely, whatever is admirable—if anything is excellent or praiseworthy—think about such things. Whatever you have learned or received or heard from me, or seen in me—put it into practice. And the God of peace will be with you."

1. Why do you think Paul was so confident in encouraging the people of the church at Philippi to put into practice the things they had received, heard, and seen in him?

    He knew that if they were preoccupied with the things that are true, noble, right, pure, lovely, and admirable, it would require that they lean on God every moment of their lives. He was confident that his example would lead them to the same source of power that he was trusting in each day of his own life.

2. What do you think is the connection between the things we are told to "think about" in verse 8 and the promise of God's "peace" in verse 9?

    These priorities keep our hearts in fellowship and our dependence on God. These things reflect God's heart. Concentrating on them as we process our daily life also keeps us from getting entangled in the things that bring turmoil, anxiety, and disappointment into our lives. They are especially helpful as we deal with difficult people and situations within our family.

1 Samuel 16:7   "But the LORD said to Samuel, 'Do not consider his appearance or his height, for I have rejected him. The LORD does not look at the things man looks at. Man looks at the outward appearance, but the LORD looks at the heart.'"

Commentary   The prophet Samuel was sent to Jesse's family to anoint one of his sons as the next king of Israel. He met the oldest son and was certain that he was the one he was to anoint as king. But God rejected the eldest son. Samuel was surprised that

God would not choose such a fine man. That's when God made this clarifying observation to him in 1 Samuel 16:7. After this, he went on to meet six more sons of Jesse, but God rejected them all. Finally he was introduced to the "baby" of the family, David, and was told to anoint him.

1. What are the things that are most often used as gauges of our spiritual life within Christian circles?

    Attendance at church activities. Service. Giving money. Bible knowledge. The way we talk. The people we spend most of our time with.

    How do they compare or contrast with the type of qualities that God looks for in us?

    God looks for the fruit of the Holy Spirit in our lives (Galatians 5:22-23). He loves it when he sees people who are committed to ideals like justice, mercy, and humility (Micah 6:8).

2. David ended up being a man with many flaws. Why do you think God still chose to anoint him as a king and spiritual leader for Israel?

    David was quick to admit when he failed. He didn't blame others. He didn't make excuses. He knew that when all was said and done, he loved God and it was his relationship with Him that was the most important part of his life (Psalm 23:1).

    What does that say about us as grandparents?

This is your opportunity to share your experience and perspective, as well as do some new thinking on our grandparenthood topic.

1. Do you think our culture's emphasis on a person's "feelings" makes it easier or more difficult to be a grandparent? In what way(s)?

    Often the right thing to do isn't always the one that feels the best. We may be frustrated by the way our children try to keep our grandchildren happy at the expense of their character. It sometimes makes it hard for us to make difficult stands with our grandchildren that we know may hurt their feelings.

2. How has the cultural shift toward "moral relativism" affected the way you make decisions and give advice as a grandparent? (Moral relativism is the assumption that "right" and "wrong" are subject to personal interpretation and are not based on any absolute standards established by God.)

    If we have surrendered to the cultural shift toward moral relativism, we may not be inclined to agree with what God says in His Word regarding certain absolute issues (like pre-marital sex, cohabitation, etc.). Relativism emphasizes things that are more temporal (i.e., looks, beauty, wealth, status, intellectual pursuits, and athletic achievements) at the expense of the things that have long-term impact. It makes it more difficult to prioritize things like hard work, honesty, and self-denial when these things get in the way of the immediate pleasures and rewards of life.

3. What are some ways we could demonstrate to our grandchildren that in spite of all of the problems that surround us as individuals, we are confident in "a mighty and sovereign God who has everything under control"?

   Not showing panic when our country finds itself in an international conflict, when elections don't go the way we would have preferred, when the economy takes a sudden and serious turn for the worse, or when we have to face serious and frightening physical setbacks.

4. Of the six character traits listed in your outline, which one do you think you most need to work on as a grand-parent? The six character traits are contagious faith, consistent integrity, practical poise, personal discipline, steadfast endurance, and inspirational courage.

   You can lead off the discussion on this one to get others to open up by sharing about the trait that you most need to work on.

Grand . . priorities

This is your opportunity to apply what you have learned in this session and become an even better grandparent.

This is the most important part of the session. Make sure you allow enough time for the participants to make personal appli-cations from what they have learned.

Questions that
make me think:

1. How has this session challenged my thinking and per-spective of grandparenthood?

   _____

   _____

   _____

2. What is one new concept or idea that comes out of this session that will change my priorities as a grandparent?

_____

_____

Actions that make me change:

1. With God's help, I will commit to making these changes in my own life:

_____

_____

2. With God's help, I will commit to the following action(s) toward those I love:

_____

_____

Make sure that you point out the Grand Promise, Grand Proverb, Grand Praise, and Grand Project at the end of this application and before you close in prayer.

Grand power

Close this session by praying for your grandchildren, especially regarding your ability to set a good standard for them to want to emulate. Ask God to help you develop a clear and uncompromised character for your grandchildren to look up to.

Grand Promise
1 Corinthians
10:31, 32

"So whether you eat or drink or whatever you do, do it all for the glory of God. Do not cause anyone to stumble..."

Grand Proverb
Proverbs 20:7

"The righteous man leads a blameless life; blessed are his children after him."

Grand Praise
Psalm 94:18, 19

"When I said, 'My foot is slipping,' your love, O LORD, supported me. When anxiety was great within me, your consolation brought joy to my soul."

Grand Power,
continued

Blessings often put burdens in perspective. Based on this session, what are some of the things for which you are thankful when it comes to your relationship with your children and grandchildren?

_____

_____

_____

_____

Grand . project

Setting a Standard

For the younger grandchildren:
Have them help you make the list of six character traits into a piece of art (you could make a bookmark, a poster, or magnets for the refrigerator). As you write out each character trait, explain to your grandchildren what it means to you or tell them about a time when that character trait helped you make a good decision.

For the older grandchildren:
Pick one of the six character traits mentioned and plan an activity with your grandchild (or a couple of your grandchildren) that focuses on developing that trait:

Faith: Plant a garden and explain how you have to exercise patience and trust in God's laws of nature.

Integrity: Take them to an ancestor's grave. If you know any anecdotes about this ancestor (positive or negative) that show how integrity (or the lack of it) affected his/her life, share it with them.

Poise: Take them to a nice restaurant and show them how ladies are to be treated (open doors, help them get seated, etc.) and how to exercise proper etiquette.

Discipline: Help them memorize an elaborate poem or passage of scripture.

Endurance: Have them open a savings account. Have them save a certain sum of money that you agree to match once they meet their goal.

Courage: Take them to a nearby war memorial or military museum and discuss the courageous people who are depicted.

(These are merely suggestions. Feel free to use your imagination and develop your own lessons for the six character traits.)

 *Grand* words

Multi-culturalism…
the belief that all cultures are worthy of study and of equal value and deserve equal celebration.

Pluralism…
the belief that all moral religions lead to God.

Moral Relativism…
the assumption that "right" and "wrong" are subject to personal interpretation and are not based on any absolute standards pre-established by God.

Poise…
a keen and balanced sense of what is appropriate in any given situation.

Recommended Reading
Raising Kids Who Turn Out Right
Home Grown Heroes
by Dr. Tim Kimmel

For a deeper look at how to transfer the character traits mentioned in this session into your grandchildren's lives, you might want to read Dr. Tim Kimmel's book, *Raising Kids Who Turn Out Right* and *Home Grown Heroes*, both available online at familymatters.net or call 800 467-4596.

Sticky Situations –
Part One

Grand focus

In our last session we learned the fourth primary role of a grandparent—setting a standard that our grandchildren would want to emulate. In this session, Tim and Darcy Kimmel are going to look at three sticky situations that complicate our roles as grandparents: when our children go through a divorce, when our grandchildren come to live with us, and how to treat the grandchildren we inherit through a blended family.

Welcome everyone. Thank them for their faithfulness to this study. Explain that in this particular lesson, they will be looking at some dilemmas that may not personally apply to them at this time. However, the principles they will be learning translate into other challenges they may be facing as grandparents. What they will learn in this lesson may also serve them in the future. This material may also help them to understand and encourage others who are facing these circumstances. Pray for God's insight as you go through this session together. Read the Grand Focus statement at the beginning of this session and then start the video/DVD.

It is important that everyone has a good view of the TV or screen and that everyone has a workbook. As the session starts, make sure that the audio is at a level that everyone can hear.

Grand principles

Please follow along with Tim and Darcy on the video/DVD and fill in the blanks as they teach. The phrases with blanks will come up on the screen.

Dealing With Divorce

A. When our children are going through a divorce we need to get perspective .

   1. We need to make a commitment to not beat ourselves up.

   2. We need to find a personal outlet for our pain .

   3. We need to ask God for objectivity .

   4. We need to keep in mind that the people who need us the most are the grandchildren .

B. When our children are going through a divorce we need to help preserve and protect a supportive relationship with our grandchildren.

1. We need to maintain _neutrality_ around them when it comes to their parents.

2. We need to be a safe place for our grandchildren to process their _emotions_ .

3. We need to help our grandchildren _heal_ .

   a. They need to consistently see evidence that proves to them that although their immediate world may look like it is falling apart, their _bigger_ world isn't.

   b. We need to concentrate on meeting the three driving inner needs we outlined in Session Two: a secure love, a significant purpose, and a sufficient hope.

   c. We need to be available to those grandchildren who need us more as they are processing their parents' divorce.

   d. We need to be positive! Don't be _grim_ . Be upbeat.

4. It's important that we protect our legal rights of access to our grandchildren.

C. We need to come alongside their _parents_ .

When Grandchildren Come to Live With Us

A. Deal with any _resentment_ you may be harboring toward their parents for putting you in this situation.

B. Make your grandchildren feel like they are in their _permanent_ home, not just visiting.

C. Don't make them feel _guilty_ .

D. Discuss with their mother and father (if they are still in the picture) what the standards of your house will be and how and who will carry out the _discipline_ .

E. Don't give up _hope_ on your grandchildren's mom and dad.

*Making the
Most of Blended
Families*

A. We need to go slowly, building a careful and patient relationship with these new grandchildren on their _timetable_ .

B. We need to ask their permission to take the relationship _deeper_ .

C. We need to start fitting them into our daily _prayer_ _time_ .

Make sure everyone has the words for the blanks in their workbook.

Grand precepts

This is an opportunity for you to dig deeper into the scriptures and be reminded of God's work in your life.

Psalm 46:1, 2 "God is our refuge and strength, an ever-present help in trouble. Therefore we will not fear, though the earth give way and the mountains fall into the heart of the sea."

1. Explain in your own words what it means for God to be your "refuge," your "strength," and your "ever-present help" as you go through difficult times with your children and grandchildren.

2. What effect does your lack of fear have on helping your children and grandchildren go through extremely difficult situations?

> Children tend to look up to the older people in their lives and put a lot of weight on their viewpoints. When they see that we aren't panicking or falling apart because we have confidence in God, they are more inspired to put their trust in Him too. It also causes them to be more inclined toward listening to our counsel

> What keeps you from trusting in God enough for Him to calm your fears?

> A small view of God. Taking our eyes off of the Lord in the midst of calamity. Lack of faith.

Isaiah 40:28-31 "Do you not know? Have you not heard? The LORD is the everlasting God, the Creator of the ends of the earth. He will not grow tired or weary, and his understanding no one can fathom. He gives strength to the weary and increases the power of the weak. Even youths grow tired and weary, and young men stumble and fall; but those who hope in the LORD will renew their strength. They will soar on wings like eagles; they will run and not grow weary, they will walk and not be faint."

1. How does the presence of an "everlasting God" and the "Creator of the ends of the earth" help keep you from caving in when your immediate world is falling apart?

> These terms refer to the sovereign power that God has exercised since the beginning of time. When we compare the size or our immediate problems against His mighty work and mighty love, it helps us maintain perspective.

2. Isaiah compares the people who find their hope in the Lord to eagles. What is it about an eagle that best illustrates the assurance that Isaiah is giving in this verse?

Eagles are not afraid to fly alone. They rise above everything. They don't have to expend a lot of energy to fly — they are borne aloft by the wind. They fly so high that a lot of the mountains and valleys start to look the same. They are not intimidated by the sheer size of the situation that we see at ground level.

This is your opportunity to share your experience and perspective, as well as do some new thinking on our grandparenthood topic.

1. What are some of the negative affects that divorce has on couples?

It causes anger, bitterness, blame, guilt, anxiety, depression, financial problems, etc. We feel powerless to change the situation. It rocks and rearranges our world in a negative way. We're afraid that we may end up with less access to our grandchildren. We somehow think it reflects negatively on us as parents. Our loyalties are challenged.

On their children?

Children feel lost in the shuffle. Some wonder if they are to blame. Children often feel that they are forced to pick between their parents—especially if a parent emotionally "plays" them against the other parent. It can cause insecurity, anxiousness, depression, 'acting out,' poor performance in school, etc.

2. How does taking sides around your grandchildren
   increase the pain and damage of a divorce?

   Because they love both parents, they feel that they have
   to defend the parent that we are criticizing. Our negative
   comments may reveal new information that causes them
   even greater insecurity about their family situation. They
   desperately need some of the adults in their lives to act
   maturely. When we pull ourselves into the middle and
   take sides around our grandchildren, they lose hope that
   any of the adults they are leaning on are reliable.

3. Even if your grandchildren only come to live with you
   for a brief period of time, how can you make them feel
   welcomed and at home?

   Be willing to put our routines aside for their best interests.
   Be willing to rearrange our social calendars. Give them
   their own space. Don't complain about their presence
   or their possessions suddenly overwhelming our homes.
   Don't be overly concerned that our possessions may get
   damaged or worn more easily, or that our houses might
   not be as clean. Welcome their friends. Show a great deal
   of grace when it comes to their music, their schedule, and
   their idiosyncrasies.

4. It's easy to say that we should love and treat all of our
   grandchildren the same—even our step-grandchildren.
   But doing it can be much more difficult. Why do you
   think this is?

   We lack a track record. We still may be holding onto the
   idea—'this should never have happened.' Our step-grandchildren may be reluctant to open up to us. They may
   openly favor their other grandparents.

What impact do you think it might have if we go out of our way to accept our "blended" grandchildren as gifts from God?

The death or divorce that placed them in this blended configuration could have done a lot of damage to their view of themselves. When they see how quickly and completely we are willing to embrace them as grandchildren, it helps them heal. It's also a great illustration of the way God treats us. When we truly believe that these grandchildren are gifts from God, it will make it easier for us to build a bridge to their hearts.

Grand priorities

This is your opportunity to apply what you have learned in this session and become an even better grandparent.

This is the most important part of the session. Make sure you allow enough time for the participants to make personal applications from what they have learned.

Questions that make me think:

1. How has this session challenged my thinking and perspective of grandparenthood?

   _____

   _____

2. What is one new concept or idea that comes out of this session that will change my priorities as a grandparent?

   _____

   _____

Actions that make me change:

1. With God's help, I will commit to making these changes in my own life:

   _____

   _____

Grand Priorities,
continued

2. With God's help, I will commit to the following action(s) toward those I love:

_____

_____

Make sure that you point out the Grand Promise, Grand Proverb, Grand Praise, and Grand Project at the end of this application and before you close in prayer.

Grand power

Close this session by praying for your children and grandchildren, especially those who may be going through difficult times in their marriage or with their finances. Ask God to help you come alongside them with the kind of help that gives them hope and relief in their difficult situations.

Grand Promise
1 Peter 5: 7, 10

"Cast all your anxiety on him because he cares for you … And the God of all grace, who called you to his eternal glory in Christ, after you have suffered a little while, will himself restore you and make you strong, firm and steadfast."

Grand Proverb
Proverbs 21:23

"He who guards his mouth and his tongue keeps himself from calamity."

Grand Praise
Lamentations
3:22, 23

"Because of the LORD's great love we are not consumed, for his compassions never fail. They are new every morning; great is your faithfulness."

Blessings often put burdens in perspective. Based on this session, what are some of the things for which you are thankful when it comes to your relationship with your children and grandchildren?

_____

_____

_____

_____

Grand project

*Sticky Situations
Part 1*

Gather all of the ingredients needed to make brownies from scratch. Have your grandchildren sample a few of the pleasant tasting ingredients as well as a few of the unpleasant tasting ingredients. After the brownies are baked, sit down to enjoy one with them. As you are eating the results of your joint effort, explain that life is like brownies. It is made up of pleasant and unpleasant parts, but God can make something good out of them. Apply this to a difficult situation they may be going through at this time.

Grand words

Objectivity…
the ability to keep your personal hurt and pain from clouding your perspective.

Step-grandchild…
someone God has brought into your life through blending or remarriage for you to love as though he or she were there from the beginning.

Sacred Trust…
the understanding that our role as grandparents is ordained by God and has eternal consequences.

Perspective…
the ability to see things from God's point of view.

Grand focus

In our last session we learned how to deal with some sticky situations that we often face, like divorce, having our grandchildren come live in our home, and the blending of families. In this session we will look at three sticky situations that all grandparents eventually deal with: the issue of spoiling, the issue of intervening on behalf of our grandchildren, and the issue of resolving conflict that naturally occurs within a family.

Welcome everyone. Explain that this is the second part of a look at some of the "sticky situations" we can find ourselves in as grandparents. Remind them that the Bible does not promise us easy lives, but it does provide us the help we need to make good choices and exercise godly strength when we are going through tough times. Grandparenting offers all of us the chance to make a huge impact in a new generation. In this session we will get an opportunity to see how to make the most of some difficult circumstances in our roles as grandparents. Pray for God's insight as you go through this session together. Read the Grand Focus statement at the beginning of this session and then start the video/DVD.

It is important that everyone has a good view of the TV or screen and that everyone has a workbook. As the session starts, make sure that the audio is at a level that everyone can hear.

Please follow along with Tim and Darcy on the video/DVD and fill in the blanks as they teach. The phrases with blanks will come up on the screen.

The Issue of Spoiling

A. Spoiling is the _natural_ outgrowth of the relationship we have with our grandchildren.

B. Spoiling is a way to _compensate_ for those earlier years of relational and financial deprivation.

C. How our children respond to our spoiling their children is based on two factors.

1. The kind of _relationship_ we had with them as they grew up.

2. The kind of _spoiling_ we're doing.

    a. Make sure that what you are doing is _okay_ with their parents.

    b. Make sure that what you are doing is _helping_ your grandchild grow into a better person.

D. For a lot of grandparents, there is a strong desire to use the money God has blessed them with to enhance their grandchildren's lives.

    1. When it comes to our money, grandchildren are better off with too _little_ of it than with too much.

    2. It is _irrelevant_ how much money we save from taxes if it ultimately goes against the best interests of our families.

    3. The better plan is to pass the money on in such a way that it helps your _children_ in their efforts to raise your grandchildren.

The Issue
of Intervention

A. There is a thin line between intervening and _interfering_ .

B. Our intervention can either empower them to be more self-sufficient and godly or it can enable them to remain in mediocrity and play the victim.

C. The best way to get results is to pray hard and live a _godly_ _life_ .

D. More direct intervention may be necessary if your grandchildren are in peril.

1. Be _proactive_ and do your best to come up with a plan that will do the most to benefit your grandchildren while leaving your sanity intact.

2. You might want to talk with an attorney and see if there is a way that you might—at least temporarily—get more legal control over your grandchildren's _daily_ lives.

E. Sometimes families have a child born to them who has a mental, physical, or developmental problem demanding a huge amount of _care_ .

The Issue of Conflict

A. Given that conflict is inevitable, our choice is in how we are going to deal with it.

B. Truth, spoken in love, in an atmosphere of forgiveness gives _grace_ a chance to work in people's hearts over time.

C. When it comes to conflict within a family, there are four things we need to keep in mind.

1. We must reject passivity as an option.

2. We must take responsibility.

3. We must lead courageously.

4. We must trust God for a greater _outcome_ .

D. In any conflict, even those that shock us, the goal is a healing that runs deep enough to touch all hearts and a _holiness_ that won't quit.

 *Grand* precepts

This is an opportunity for you to dig deeper into the scriptures and be reminded of God's work in your life.

Make sure everyone has the words for the blanks in their workbooks.

Ephesians 3:17b-21 "And I pray that you, being rooted and established in love, may have power, together with all the saints to grasp how wide and long and high and deep is the love of Christ, and to know this love that surpasses knowledge—that you may be filled to the measure of all the fullness of God. Now to him who is able to do immeasurably more than all we ask or imagine, according to his power that is at work within us, to him be glory in the church and in Christ Jesus throughout all generations, for ever and ever! Amen."

1. Do you think these verses hint that God likes to spoil His children? (See the definition of "spoiling" in Grand Words.)

    Some may have a difficult time attributing the word "spoiling" to God. That's why it is important to establish the definition from the Grand Words first. Point out that there is good spoiling and bad spoiling. God's desire to lavish us with His blessings comes from His enormous love for us.

    According to these verses, what are some of the ways that God lavishes His love on His children?

    He does more than we can measure, more than we ask, and more than we can even imagine.

2. What does this passage say is a prerequisite to appreciating God's "spoiling" love?

    We need to first be established (grounded, confident, unwavering) in God's love.

How does that look for a Christian?

We need to avoid the legalistic view that teaches us that God's love is based on our obedience. The truth is, His love is unconditional. We enjoy God's spoiling love when we operate without any doubts of His goodness—confident in His grace. Our disobedience may block some of His *blessings*, but it never blocks His *love* for us.

Colossians 3:16, 17   "Let the word of Christ dwell in you richly as you teach and admonish one another with all wisdom, and as you sing psalms, hymns and spiritual songs with gratitude in your hearts to God. And whatever you do, whether in word or deed, do it all in the name of the Lord Jesus, giving thanks to God the Father through him."

1. During a time of intervention or conflict, where should our advice or wisdom have its source?

    It should come from the "word of Christ"—the Bible.

    Why does this make a difference in our relationships?

    Basing our advice and wisdom on His Word is more likely to keep our pride and personal opinions in check. It holds us back from operating in a selfish mode.

2. When we handle difficult situations with our children and grandchildren, with a commitment to "do it all in the name of the Lord Jesus, giving thanks to God," how does that affect the outcome?

    It helps us see the person(s) we're dealing with through the eyes of God's grace. It keeps us from letting our anger or disappointment in them get the best of us. We're more likely to desire a peaceful outcome than revenge.

Grand discussion

This is your opportunity to share your experience and perspective, as well as do some new thinking on our grandparenthood topic.

1. When does spoiling go from being a positive factor in our relationship with our children and grandchildren to a negative one?

    When we undermine their parents' authority or personal wishes. When we focus our spoiling on one grandchild or one family at the expense of the others. When we are building a sense of entitlement into our grandchildren. When we are using it to buy their love or loyalty.

2. Have you experienced tension when it comes to how much you help your children financially? Have you found a workable balance when it comes to offering a helping hand financially? If so, how?

    The key is helping without hurting. We want to make sure that we don't undermine the key breadwinner's role, we don't remove motivation for hard work, we don't give grandchildren more money than they are mature enough to handle, and we give equally and reasonably.

3. Have you been able to see any patterns in the kinds of help that your children tend to receive well and the kinds that they don't? Share about what you've learned.

    Some children may resent any help that is not asked for first. Some may receive physical help with some task or need and not financial assistance. Others may only receive help in the form of a loan. Sometimes it might depend on what mood he or she is in at the time of the offering.

4. In our session, Dr. Kimmel said, "In any conflict, even those that shock us, the goal is a healing that runs deep enough to touch all hearts and a holiness that won't quit." When it comes to rejecting passivity, taking responsibility, leading courageously, and trusting God for a greater outcome, which one of these do you struggle most with during a conflict? What do you think you could do to contribute to the healing and resolution during a time of conflict with your children or grandchildren?

We need to become accountable to friends in the area of our weaknesses. We need to get people to pray for us. We need to be vulnerable with our children about our needing to work to be better contributors to peace. We need to ask God for the grace to overcome our wrong patterns of dealing with conflict—if for no other reason than the fact that our grandchildren's lives can be severely affected.

Grand . .
priorities

This is your opportunity to apply what you have learned in this session and become an even better grandparent.

This is the most important part of the session. Make sure you allow enough time for the participants to make personal applications from what they have learned.

Questions that make me think:

1. How has this session challenged my thinking and perspective of grandparenthood?

   _____

   _____

2. What is one new concept or idea that comes out of this session that will change my priorities as a grandparent?

   _____

   _____

Actions that 1. With God's help, I will commit to making these changes
make me change: in my own life:

_____

_____

2. With God's help, I will commit to the following action(s)
   toward those I love:

_____

_____

Make sure that you point out the Grand Promise, Grand
Proverb, Grand Praise, and Grand Project at the end of this
application and before you close in prayer.

Grand power

*Close this session by praying for your grandchildren, especially
regarding your ability to set a good standard for them to want
to emulate. Ask God to help you have a clear and uncompromised character for your grandchildren to look up to.*

Grand Promise
Isaiah 41:10

"So do not fear, for I am with you; do not be dismayed, for
I am your God. I will strengthen you and help you; I will
uphold you with my righteous right hand."

Grand Proverb
Proverbs 11:25

"A generous man will prosper; he who refreshes others will
himself be refreshed."

Grand Praise
Philippians 4:6, 7

"Do not be anxious about anything, but in everything, by prayer
and petition, with thanksgiving, present your requests to God.
And the peace of God, which transcends all understanding, will
guard your hearts and your minds in Christ Jesus."

Blessings often put burdens in perspective. Based on this session,
what are some of the things for which you are thankful when it
comes to your relationship with your children and grandchildren?

_____

_____

_____

_____

Grand project

Sticky Situations
Part 2

Ask your grandchildren to describe a "dream come true" day. Although you may not be able to make all of those dreams come true (and after getting the 'okay' from their parents), do what you can to spoil them just a little bit with a day of their kind of fun.

Grand words

Spoiling…
a generosity that is the natural outgrowth of the affinity between those who love and those who are loved.

Inheritance…
the tangible and intangible assets we want to bequeath to the next generation that empowers them to love and serve God more effectively.

Intervention…
stepping in to help or protect people who aren't in the best position to help or protect themselves.

Interference…
unsolicited intervention or assistance that enables the people we love to remain in a state of mediocrity or view themselves as victims.

Recommended
Reading

How To Deal With Powerful Personalities
Little House on the Freeway
by Dr. Tim Kimmel

For a deeper look at how to bring the best out of difficult and controlling personalities in your family, you might want to read Dr. Tim Kimmel's book, *How to Deal With Powerful Personalities*. To maintain calm and rest in your hurried families, you might want to read *Little House on the Freeway*, also by Dr. Tim Kimmel. Both books are available online at www.familymatters.net or call 800 467- 4596.

Rock-n-Roll
Grandparents

SESSION 8

Grand focus

In our last session we learned how to deal with some sticky situations that we often face as grandparents, such as spoiling our grandchildren, intervening on their behalf, and being a peacemaker. In this session we will look at how to reformat some parts of our lives to the best interests of our grandchildren and how to bring the best out of them as they grow older. We'll close off with a reminder of the strategic role we play in impacting the next generations.

Welcome everyone. Remind them that this is the last session in the video study. Thank them for their participation and the contributions they have made through their involvement. Pray for God's insight as you go through this session together. Read the Grand Focus statement at the beginning of this session and then start the video/DVD.

It is important that everyone has a good view of the TV or screen and that everyone has a workbook. As the session starts, make sure that the audio is at a level that everyone can hear.

Grand principles

Please follow along with Tim and Darcy on the video/DVD and fill in the blanks as they teach. The phrases with blanks will come up on the screen.

Welcoming Our Grandchildren Into Our Home

A. We need to retrofit our surroundings to make them _safe_ for our grandchildren.

B. Often we will be called on to babysit our grandchildren.

1. We should know their schedules, their individual needs, and the special ways our grandchildren like things to happen.

2. We need to have a clear strategy on how we deal with them when they _disobey_ .

3. We should not use our time with them to _override_ any quirky parenting styles that we don't agree with.

4. When it comes to babysitting, we need to tell our children how often and how long we are available to babysit and then let them decide how they want to schedule that time.

Grand Principles, C. When our grandchildren come to our home, it is important
continued   to have a plan for how we will occupy them and have
                   <u>fun</u> with them.

D. When our grandchildren become teenagers we need
   to be committed to maintaining a connection to their
   <u>spirits</u> during this fragile and exciting time
   in their development.

   1. Their teenage years are a good time for us to focus
      on their hearts, not their hair; on their character,
      not their clothing.

   2. This is a time to spend more <u>resources</u> on them
      (special adventures, shopping, transporting them
      to events, making your home available to them for
      special occasions).

   3. They need someone who is a safe harbor for their
      inner <u>worries</u> (peer pressure, sexual temptation,
      fears of inadequacy).

Our Most   A. We need to pray for them every day.
Important Role:
Showing Them   B. We need to pray that they will have tender hearts
the Way to God   to the gospel.

C. We need to pray that they will have gracious hearts
   to the people around them.

D. We need to pray that they will have willing hearts to
   <u>respond</u> to God's truth as it is revealed to them.

The Grandparent's Prayer

Dear Heavenly Father, thank you for creating families, and thank you especially for the gift of my grandchildren. I pray that you would protect and prepare them morally, physically, emotionally, intellectually, and spiritually. I offer myself to be used by you in the lives of my grandchildren to bless them, to light the way, to be a good example, and to leave a legacy through them that lasts forever. Amen.

Make sure everyone has the words for the blanks in their workbooks.

Grand precepts

This is an opportunity for you to dig deeper into the scriptures and be reminded of God's work in your life.

I Kings 11:4

"As Solomon grew old, his wives turned his heart after other gods, and his heart was not fully devoted to the LORD his God, as the heart of David his father had been."

1. Based on what you know about King Solomon, why do you think he was vulnerable to compromise and unfaithfulness as he grew older?

   He lived a self-indulgent lifestyle. He was half-hearted in his commitment to God. He allowed nonbelievers to affect his thinking. He got lazy and apathetic about the eternal issues.

2. What were the qualities of King David that kept him strong to the end?

   He was quick to humble himself before God. He admitted his faults and mistakes. He did not make excuses. He lived a life that forced him to trust in God. He maintained honesty with God. He spent a lot of his time praising God.

Isaiah 62:6, 7   "I have posted watchmen on your walls, O Jerusalem; they will never be silent day or night. You who call on the LORD, give yourselves no rest, and give him no rest till he establishes Jerusalem and makes her the praise of the earth."

1. Why do you think the watchmen were called on to also pray?

    The families in the city were completely at the mercy of the watchmen. If the watchmen didn't do their job, these people could easily be overcome. The fact that there were innocent people depending on them had a sobering effect on the watchmen. It reminded them that their job was bigger than themselves and they needed divine help to carry it out. Prayer was the logical response to the vulnerability that they faced.

    What relationship does that have to our roles as grandparents?

    The fact that there are innocent people depending on us has a sobering effect on us. We realize how dependent we are on God. We've lived long enough to realize how many dangers and threats are lurking in the shadows of day-to-day life. We need to be praying on behalf of our grandchildren who may still be helpless or naïve about what they are dealing with.

2. When you read, "give yourselves no rest, and give Him no rest ..." what does that tell you about how we should be praying as grandparents?

    Prayer needs to be more than a convenient exercise in our lives. We need to deliberately and passionately go to God with our requests on behalf of our grandchildren. James 5:16b says, "The prayer of a righteous man is powerful and effective." God doesn't mind us being persistent. For further biblical reference on this issue of persistent prayer, look at Luke 11:5–10; 18:1–8.

This is your opportunity to share your experience and perspective, as well as do some new thinking on our grandparenthood topic.

1. How has your relationship with your grandchildren changed as they've grown?

   There will be many answers to this question. Some might say that their relationships have improved. Others might say just the opposite. Ask them what they are doing to enhance their roles as assets to their grandchildren.

2. What do you think is the biggest contribution you can make to your grandchildren as a grandparent?

   They might want to answer this looking at their grandchildren as a whole or by considering them individually.

3. What are the biggest obstacles to your being the kind of grandparent you'd like to be?

   Make sure the discussion stays focused on what the participants can do. Avoid letting this discussion get into blaming others for their problems.

4. What is the most important lesson you've learned from this study on grandparenthood?

   Encourage them to consider the entire set of eight sessions. There might be a great lesson they learned in one of the earlier parts of the study that is already paying off for them. This is a great time for people to tell what God is doing in their lives as grandparents as a result of working through this series.

Important: *Before you finish this session and the entire study, please turn to your evaluation on page 97 (participant's page 73) and give us your valuable feedback on Grandparenthood—More than Rocking Chairs.*

This is a very important part of helping us make Grandparenthood – More than Rocking Chairs the best tool it can be for grandparents. Please lead the participants through the evaluation and then collect them all and fax them to 480 948-7704 or mail them to:

Family Matters™
P.O. Box 14382
Scottsdale, AZ 85267

Remind them to include their full name and address so that we can mail them their special reminder gift of Grandparenthood – More than Rocking Chairs.

Grand . . priorities

This is your opportunity to apply what you have learned in this session and become an even better grandparent.

This is the most important part of the session. Make sure you allow enough time for the participants to make personal applications from what they have learned.

Questions that make me think:

1. How has this session challenged my thinking and perspective of grandparenthood?

   _____

   _____

2. What is one new concept or idea that comes out of this session that will change my priorities as a grandparent?

   _____

   _____

Actions that
make me change:

1. With God's help, I will commit to making these changes in my own life:

   _____

   _____

2. With God's help, I will commit to the following action(s) toward those I love:

   _____

   _____

Make sure that you point out the Grand Promise, Grand Proverb, Grand Praise, and Grand Project at the end of this application and before you close in prayer.

Grand power

Close this session by praying for your grandchildren, especially for the impact you have in their lives as you personally interact with them. Ask God for a special measure of His grace as you use your influence in their lives to show them the way to put their complete confidence in Jesus Christ.

Grand Promise
Galatians 5:22, 23

"But the fruit of the Spirit is love, joy, peace, patience, kindness, goodness, faithfulness, gentleness and self-control."

Grand Proverb
Proverbs 17:6

"Children's children are a crown to the aged, and parents are the pride of their children."

Grand Praise
Psalm 112:1, 2

"Praise the LORD. Blessed is the man who fears the LORD, who finds great delight in his commands. His children will be mighty in the land; the generation of the upright will be blessed."

Grand Power,
continued
Blessings often put burdens in perspective. Based on this session, what are some of the things for which you are thankful when it comes to your relationship with your children and grandchildren?

_____

_____

_____

_____

Grand project

Rock-n-Roll
Grandparents

Look back over your "Grand Priorities: Actions That Make Me Change" section of the last eight lessons and pick three specific action points that you want to start working on immediately. Take a moment right now to "time activate" those action points. Tell a friend about the specific actions you want to take to be a more effective grandparent and ask them to pray for you and hold you accountable.

In Appreciation
Reminders help all of us live our lives more effectively. To receive your special reminder of your study of *Grandparenthood —More Than Rocking Chairs*, please fill out the evaluation in the back of your workbook and send it to Family Matters. We value your feedback and we would love to send you a special grandparenting keepsake.

Grand challenge

One of the ways you can make a difference is by leading another group of grandparents through this video study. It might be people in your church, your neighbors, or friends with whom you share a hobby or common interest.

Ideas for formats:
A grandparents' Sunday school class
A grandparents' retreat
A weekly breakfast or luncheon series
A home fellowship study
A Sunday evening series

Grand Challenge,
continued

Another way is to encourage your church to start Grand-parenting groups and use this video study. You might want to pass the word on to other grandparents you know about how this video series has made a difference in your life. For more information about Family Matters or how to get more workbooks for your next study go to grandparenthood.net or call 800 467- 4596.

Grand words

Teenagers…
wonderful young people who need patient grandparents to help them pass successfully through the corridor of adolescence.

Grandfather…
someone who has pictures where his money used to be.

Grandmother…
someone who is "full" when there is only one cookie left on the plate.

Babysitting…
an opportunity for our children to finally get even with us.

Recommended
Reading

Grace-Based Parenting
By Dr. Tim Kimmel

For a deeper look at how to love your grandchildren the way God loves us, you might want to read Dr. Tim Kimmel's book, *Grace-Based Parenting*, available at your local bookstore and online at www.familymatters.net or call 800 467- 4596.

About
Family Matters

with Dr. Tim Kimmel

Family Matters is a non-profit ministry whose goal is to see families transformed by God into instruments of restoration and reformation by equipping families for every age and stage of life. We view families as the foundation of a successful society. Today, perhaps more than ever before, the family is being fragmented and undermined by many counter-forces such as busyness, relentless change, a lack of clear moral values, an attitude of indifference, and children being forced to grow up too fast. When families are unhealthy, our communities suffer many of the consequences in areas relating to economic productivity, education, law enforcement, health care needs, abuse, and violence.

Family Matters offers hope to today's family by…

— Educating family members about the strategic role they play in their homes and communities.

— Equipping family members with successful relational skills and resources to make better family choices.

— Encouraging family members to keep their promises and fulfill their commitments to one another.

In addition to offering hope, our ministry philosophy embraces a grace-based approach to relationships, provides a solid grasp of the "big picture," promotes a character-driven strategy for parenting, and shows family members how to leave a legacy that never dies.

Family Matters has created many relevant, practical and well-researched tools to equip families. See the Resources section in this workbook or visit our web site at www.familymatters.net, for the books, video series and conferences developed by Dr. Tim and Darcy Kimmel.

Little House On The Freeway

Do you need rest for your hurried home? *Little House on the Freeway* offers biblical insights and principles for our hurried existence by teaching practical ways to deal with real life pressures that can rob us of our joy. Learn how to steer clear of unhealthy stress and toward family closeness by restoring calm to your family, marriage, and relationship with God.

Basic Training For A Few Good Men

It's easy to be a man, but it's hard to be a good one. The playing field isn't level and most of the hopes that boys bring to manhood are dashed before they reach middle age. In *Basic Training For a Few Good Men*, Dr. Kimmel restores hope by teaching life-changing principles through real-life stories with a wit and a punch that make you eager to see what's on the next page.

How To Deal With Powerful Personalities

Dr. Tim Kimmel looks at the high cost of high control by helping you understand the types and causes of controlling behavior, from passive manipulation to aggressive control. You will learn how to break free from the pain caused by controlling personalities—your own and others'—and develop or restore secure, lasting relationships.

Raising Kids Who Turn Out Right

Every parent hopes their kids will turn out right. There are no shortcuts to successful parenting, however; there are steps you can take to prepare your children for the challenges ahead. With warmth and conviction Dr. Tim Kimmel outlines a strategy for positive parenting—a plan that gives you reachable goals, while allowing for your personal parenting style.

Four Biblical Roles of Parenting and Grandparenting

These booklets provide an easy reference for remembering the most important goals in parenting/grandparenting.

Grace Based Parenting

Too much of today's Christian parenting is based on fear. Grace based parenting relies on God's love, replicates His forgiveness and displaces fear as a motivator for every behavior. Grace Based Parenting will show you how to love your children the way God loves His – with grace.

Home Grown Heroes

The choices your children face are much tougher than the ones you wrestled with. They are going to need courage. Through inspiring stories, practical teaching, and hefty doses of common sense, veteran family advocate Dr. Tim Kimmel charts a course your family can follow. It's the most strategic investment you may ever make.

Little House On The Freeway Home Maintenance Manual: 301 Ways To Bring Rest To Your Hurried Home

Families today struggle to spend time together. But even in the midst of the most frenzied schedules you can find ways to bring rest to your hurried home. You'll find 301 helpful and creative suggestions inside to help you build up the relationships within your family.

Surviving Life In The Fast Lane

If your life has gotten a little too fast and furious, here's a way to slow down without crashing. *Surviving Life in the Fast Lane* will help you restore calmness, focus, and rest to your family life, marriage, friendships, work situation, and—most importantly—your relationship with God in a study guide format.

To order or find out more about these and other resources, go to www.familymatters.net and click on "Resources," or call 800 467-4596.

Hurried Family Video Series

Our fast-paced American society promotes a constant drive for success, but often at the expense of our inner peace and contentment. "The increase of information, transportation and contamination have cost us dearly," says Dr. Tim Kimmel. "Our sense of permanence, unity and peace are jeopardized by hurried lifestyles." Based on his best selling book, *Little House on the Freeway*, Tim Kimmel brings help to the hurried home by sharing positive ways to overcome one's hectic lifestyle. In ten sessions with practical applications, *The Hurried Family Video Series* explores the symptoms of a hurried family and provides counsel for restoring calmness and giving the gift of rest to others.

Raising Kids Who Turn Out Right Video Series

This video series provides a strategy for positive parenting goals, while allowing for your personal parenting style. There are steps you can take to prepare your children for the challenges ahead, but you will need an effective game plan. This is an excellent tool for individuals, as well as small groups and Sunday School classes. It includes eight powerful video sessions, study guide and facilitator's guide. A CD-ROM provides an overview of the entire study, including teaching helps and promotion suggestions that enable the facilitator to lead this series with confidence.

Basic Training For a Few Good Men Video Series

Basic Training presents scriptural principles to empower men to "stand in the gap" and be "watchmen on the wall" before the Lord for their families. The challenges that men are facing in our culture today are staggering. Many men feel lost, without a solid moral compass. They feel helpless as to what position they are to play in a society that is constantly changing. *Basic Training* is a crash course in character. It's a no holds barred study of the things that turn men of faith into men of God. This exciting study includes how men can flourish at work, draw the best out of their wives, make it easy for their kids to look up to them, and find it a joy to serve in God's army.

Grandparent's Prayer Journal

Grandchild's Name _____

Prayer Request _____

_____

_____

_____

Answer _____

_____

Grandchild's Name _____

Prayer Request _____

_____

_____

_____

Answer _____

_____

Grandchild's Name _____

Prayer Request _____

_____

_____

_____

Answer _____

_____

Grandchild's Name _____

Prayer Request _____

_____

_____

_____

Answer _____

_____

Feel free to make as many copies of this Prayer Journal as you need.

Evaluation Name _____

Address _____

Email _____

Phone number _____

Please mail or fax your evaluation to:

Family Matters
P.O. Box 14382
Scottsdale, AZ
85267

fax:
480.948.7704

We appreciate your feedback to help us do our job more effectively and participate in the blessing of changed lives.

Your comments may be an encouragement to others. However, if you do NOT wish to have your comments shared anonymously with others, please check here ☐

1. As a result of going through *Grandparenthood—More than Rocking Chairs*, how have you changed as a grandparent?

    _____
    _____
    _____

2. What are three new ideas or concepts that you learned from this study?

    _____
    _____
    _____

3. How are your grandchildren going to benefit by you going through this study?

    _____
    _____
    _____

4. Take a few moments to share how God is using you in your family to give a blessing, leave a legacy, bear a torch, or set a standard.

    _____
    _____
    _____

5. Has facilitating this study been a positive experience? How or Why?

_____

_____

_____

6. What are a few ways that you have observed the grandparents in your group maturing in their roles and responsibilities to their families?

_____

_____

_____

7. Is there a story or two that you could share with us about lives being affected by your group study and discussion?

_____

_____

_____

8. Is there any other feedback you would like to give Tim or Darcy Kimmel or Family Matters regarding the video/DVD lessons, the Facilitator's Guide, the Participant's Workbook or the CD-Rom?

_____

_____

_____

Thank you for taking the time to fill out this evaluation.

When you mail or fax this form to Family Matters,™ we would like to show our appreciation for your feedback by sending you a special reminder of your study of *Grandparenthood — More than Rocking Chairs*.

Thank you.